To:

From:

Words of Encouragement

Written and compiled by
Margolyn Woods and Maureen MacLellan

Illustrated by Anne Smith

INSPIRE

Inspire Books is an imprint
of Peter Pauper Press, Inc.

Spire is a registered trademark of Peter Pauper Press, Inc.

For our children: Sherrilynn, Bryan, Nicolle,
Robyn, Bekki, Taryn, Matthew, and Adam
Thank you for encouraging and enriching our lives.

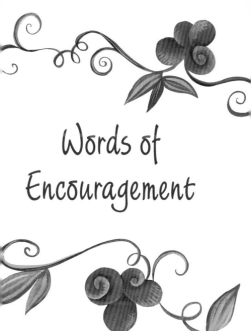

Words of
Encouragement

Introduction

For years we have posted WORDS OF
ENCOURAGEMENT around our homes, on our
refrigerators and desks, and on our mirrors.
Upon finding a new saying that warms
our hearts or uplifts us, we immediately
share this new treasure with each other.

It is our hope that you will be encouraged
and uplifted with these WORDS OF
ENCOURAGEMENT and pass them
on to your own friends and family.

M. W. and M. M.

therefore encourage one another,

and build up one another . . .

1 Thessalonians 5:11 NASB

When the world
gets you down,
look up to God.

Expect a Miracle.

People don't care
that you know,
until they know
that you care!

Good morning!

This is God! I will be handling all of your problems today. I will not need your help. So have a good day.

Before you put on your
clothes for the day, put
on a good attitude;
everything will fit
better.

People may not remember
exactly what you did, or
what you said—
but they will remember
how you made them feel.

Never accept
unacceptable behavior,
or you make
it acceptable.

Here is the test to find
out if your mission
on earth is finished: if
you're alive, it isn't.

Richard Bach

Every disappointment
or challenge
is an opportunity
for growth.

Another meaning for A.S.A.P.
is "Always Say A Prayer."
God knows how stressful life is.
He wants to ease our cares.
Slow down and take a breather—
always say a prayer.

There are good ships and wood ships,
And ships that sail the seven seas,
But the best ships
are friendships
And may they always be.

Trust grows from
trustworthiness.

When you don't
know what to do,
pray.

You cannot discover new oceans unless you have the courage to lose sight of the shore.

See where God is working and join Him in that work.

If a problem lasts all
month it's only
1/960th of your life.
Keep your perspective!

Do your best;
let God
do the rest.

Growing old
is mandatory;
growing up is
optional.

Many people will walk
in and out of your life,
but only true friends
will leave footprints
in your heart.

Eleanor Roosevelt

The company you
keep will
determine the
trouble you meet.

Think this
is too big for
God to handle?

Remember, people who try to whittle you down are only trying to reduce you to their size.

Those who
deserve love the
least need it
the most.

Peace is not the
absence of trouble,
but the presence
of God.

The best way to
get the last word
is to apologize.

Thoughtful minds
discuss events;
thoughtless minds
discuss people.

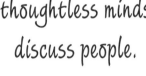

Coincidence is
when God chooses
to remain
anonymous.

Does it glorify God?

He who loses money
loses much.
He who loses a friend
loses much more.
He who loses faith loses all.

To handle yourself,
use your head;
to handle others,
use your heart.

Learn from the mistakes of others. You can't live long enough to make them all yourself.

Friends are angels who lift us to our feet when our wings have trouble remembering how to fly.

May the best day
of your past be the
worst day of
your future.

Today, instead of
telling God how big
your problem is, tell your
problem how big God is!

Mother Teresa was once
asked if she wished she had done
more, to which she replied,
"God called me to be faithful,
not successful."

You fail only when
you quit trying.

The light that shines
the farthest is the light
that is strongest at
its source.

May there always be work for
your hands to do;
May your purse always
hold a coin or two;
May the sun always shine
on your windowpane;
May a rainbow be certain
to follow each rain;
May the hand of a friend always
be near you;
May God fill your heart with
gladness to cheer you.

God gives His best
to those who give
Him control.

Keep the SON

in your eyes!

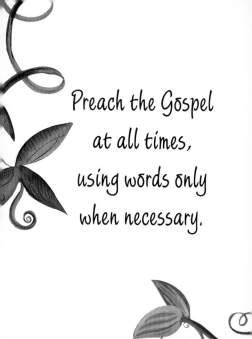

Preach the Gospel
at all times,
using words only
when necessary.

The problem you are dealing with is just a stage you are passing through. It will be much easier to look at in the rear view mirror than it is in the headlights.

Are you busy feathering your nest, or furthering His Kingdom?

When your identity
comes from being a child
of God, you become a
secure person.

What did you
do with what
He gave you?

Sometimes
personal growth hurts.
Have you ever heard
the term "growing pains"?
Try focusing on the
"growing" part.

Remember, some of
God's greatest gifts
are unanswered
prayers.

This is the day which
the LORD has made;
Let us rejoice and
be glad in it.

Psalms 118:24 NASB

The shortest distance between a problem and the solution is the distance between your knees and the floor.

The one who
kneels to the Lord
can stand up to
anything.

Redemption is not
an exemption
from difficulties.

The easiest way to feel good is to say something kind to someone else.

What part of
"Thou shalt not . . ."
don't you
understand?

Whatever you do,
make sure it has God's
fingerprints all over it.

The secret of
success is
consistency of
purpose.

Determination is often
the first chapter in the
book of excellence.

I am not what I want
to be. I am not what
I ought to be.
But, thank God
I am not what I was!

God Himself does not
propose to judge a
man 'til he is dead.
So why should we?

For a slim figure, share
your food with the hungry.
For lovely eyes, seek out the good
in people. For an attractive face,
speak words of kindness. For
poise, walk with the knowledge
that you never walk alone.

Audrey Hepburn

God delights in me.
He wants to be with me.
He waits for me to
wake up each day!

Always laugh,
always hug, always love,
always pray.

Karen Covell

What happens
to men and women
is less significant
than what happens
within them.

Every child of God is a
treasure, but often
I forget I'm one of
those precious gems.

Louise Tucker Jones

The task ahead
of you is never
greater than the
power behind you.

Exercise daily—
walk with
the Lord.

God grades on
the cross,
not on the curve.

When God ordains,
He sustains.

An individual can succeed at almost anything for which he has unlimited enthusiasm.

Be ye fishers of men.
You catch them—
He will clean them.

All glory comes
from daring
to begin.

God doesn't call
the qualified—
He qualifies
the called.

Kindness is difficult to give away, because it keeps coming back.

Margolyn Woods is a former Rose Bowl Queen and actress who now lives on a farm just outside of Oklahoma City She is a popular speaker at women's retreats.

Maureen MacLellan has worked in the health care industry for many years. She owns a medical marketing and management company in Orange County, California. She resides in Huntington Beach.

Margolyn and Maureen are sisters and best friends.